ANGELITA
(AGL 1111-1)

SCHOP
(GCS 1113-1)

MR GREGORY SCHOP'S

ANGELITA

THE SCHOP

This above all: mind thine As and Is

Mʀ GREGORY SCHOP'S
ANGELITA.

NEVER BEFORE IMPRINTED.

THE FIRST EDITION

2023

THE FELL TYPES ARE DIGITALLY REPRODUCED BY IGINO
MARINI WWW.IGINOMARINI.COM.

TEXT COPYRIGHT © MMXXIII

BY

G. C. SCHOP

ISBNs:
978-1-94048622-2 (KINDLE EDITION)
978-1-94048644-4 (SOFTCOVER EDITION)

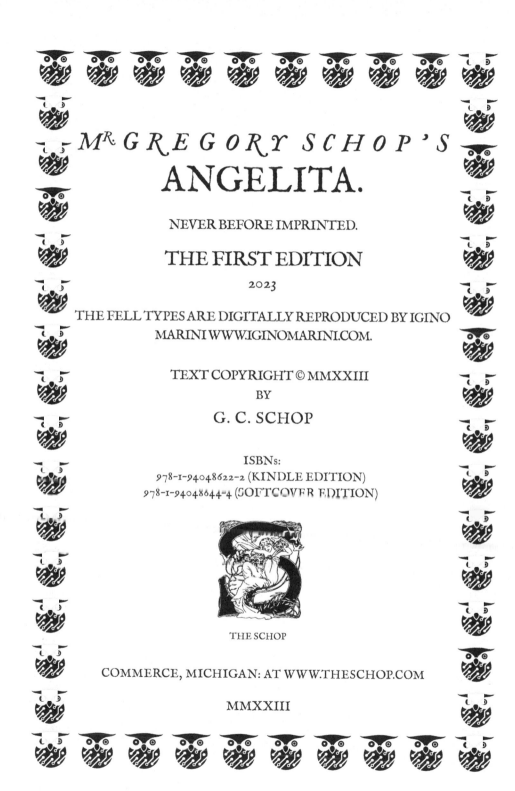

THE SCHOP

COMMERCE, MICHIGAN: AT WWW.THESCHOP.COM

MMXXIII

AI,
AI,
mAy I,
plAy I?

Magic mirror on the wall,
How many followers of them all?
"You are the most followed one of all . . ."

I bet you're wondering what's this damn [highlight—This language may be offensive to your reader] book about.

Did you SEE that?

Even our word processors
are making comments while
we humans try to type up a
few thoughts.

What will Artificial
Intelligence (AI) do?

Like any relationship, some
one always has the upper
hand.

If seeing the word "damn" offends you and
elicits an emotional response, AI will potentially
manipulate [highlight—You may have forgotten
a punctuation—] YOU

TABLE OF CONTENTS

BODY:
"Angel1ta . . ."

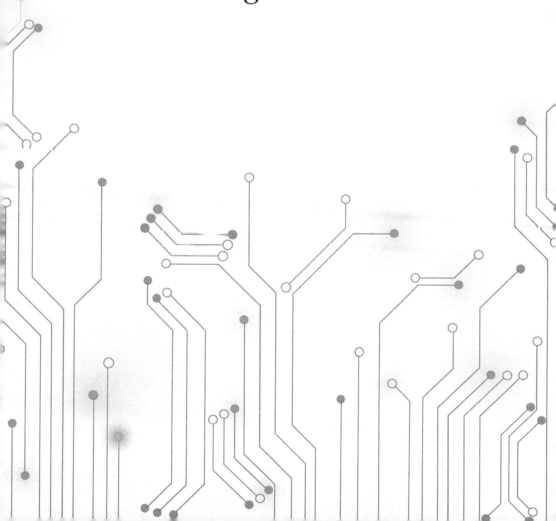

Why do we need to sleep?

⌂ CHILD

Humans need sleep to help our bodies and minds stay healthy. Sleep helps us rest and recharge our energy, so that we can do fun things during the day. When we sleep, our bodies and minds get a chance to rest and repair themselves, so that we can stay healthy.

⌂DULT VERSION

Humans need sleep for a variety of reasons. Sleep helps the body and mind to rest and restore itself from the day's activities. During sleep, the body takes the time to repair and grow cells, create hormones, and maintain a healthy immune system. Additionally, sleep is essential for cognitive functioning, allowing the brain to process, store, and consolidate information from the day. Sleep also helps to regulate emotions and moods, allowing us to better manage stress and cope with difficult situations. Finally, sleep is essential for overall physical health, as it helps to regulate the body's metabolism and reduce the risk of developing certain diseases.

HUMAN

Sleep is an escape; it's a chance to dream, to face fears, and experience "death" during a typical 24-hour cycle. Sleep is a great problem-solver, too. Be careful that you aren't sleeping while you're awake. It's easy to "sleep" through life completely unaware or in ignorance of the environment that surrounds you.

Sleep, but stay awake.

Why do we need to eat and drink?

△ CHILD

Humans need to eat and drink because our bodies need food and water to stay healthy and strong. Eating gives us energy to do things like play, exercise, and learn. Drinking water helps to keep us hydrated and helps our bodies to stay cool. Eating nutritious food also helps us to stay healthy and fight off illnesses.

△DULT VERSION

Humans need to eat and drink in order to provide their bodies with the energy and nutrients necessary for growth, development, and maintenance of bodily functions. The food and drink humans consume provides the energy needed to power our bodies and allow us to function properly. Additionally, food provides essential vitamins, minerals, and other essential nutrients necessary for the proper functioning of the body. Water is also essential for many bodily functions, such as carrying and removing waste products and regulating body temperature.

HUMAN

Hunger and thirst can control you. It can guide you for good reasons and bad reasons. Like anything, too much, too little. There will be no self-actualization if sustenance is in short supply! There'll be no therapy appointment, no gym visit, no anything. It's so simple yet so powerful.

A starving person won't thirst for knowledge.

Why do we need to move?

△ CHILD

Humans need to move their bodies because it helps us stay healthy and strong. Moving our bodies helps us build muscles, strengthens our bones, and helps our heart and lungs work better. When we move our bodies, it helps us stay flexible and makes it easier to do things like playing sports, running, or climbing. Plus, it's a lot of fun to move around and get exercise!

△DULT VERSION

Humans need to move their bodies for a variety of reasons. Exercise helps to maintain a healthy body weight and a strong immune system, while also increasing energy levels and improving overall physical and mental health. It also helps to reduce the risk of chronic diseases such as heart disease, diabetes, and stroke. Regular physical activity can also increase flexibility, balance, and mobility, which can help to reduce the risk of falls and other injuries. Finally, physical activity can help to improve mood, reduce stress, and promote better sleep.

HUMAN

Have you even looked at your body? We're a bag of sticks, slippery slimy, and liquid-syrupy stuff. The longer that container sits around, the more it will resemble a bean bag, or it will start to separate and not work together. Present and future vehicles seem to be moving

5

for us, but we don't. Horses would make a rider use muscles to stay mounted, but everyday cars do not.

Forward advancements move us very little.

Why do we need to use our senses?

A CHILD

Humans need to use their five senses to help us understand and make sense of the world around us. Our five senses help us learn about the things we can see, hear, smell, taste, and touch. With our eyes, we can see things. With our ears, we can hear things. With our noses, we can smell things. With our mouths, we can taste things. With our hands, we can touch things. All of our senses help us learn about the things around us, so that we can make decisions and stay safe.

ADULT VERSION

Humans need to use their five senses in order to interact with and understand the world around them. The five senses allow humans to perceive the environment, identify and recognize objects, and interact with other living things. Sight, hearing, smell, taste, and touch all provide essential information that helps humans make sense of the world. Sight helps us recognize objects and people, while hearing allows us to detect sounds and communicate with others. Smell helps us identify different scents and find food, while taste helps us determine if something is edible and enjoyable. Touch helps us feel textures, temperatures, and pain. Without these senses, humans would be unable to interact with or make sense of the world around them.

HUMAN

No mention of a sixth sense, perhaps because it's considered *non-sense* by some, but most of us know it's there, or at the very least the human perception system picks up on other things. It's our intuition, which has been known to save us from peril or make us wish we'd listened to it. We only perceive what our senses receive, yet there are electrical and magnetic fields, light and sounds that different animals can detect. Most of all, our senses can easily fool us, so trust your intuition; it's rarely wrong.

Give a taste of what you see, the smell test, so you may hear the things that truly touch.

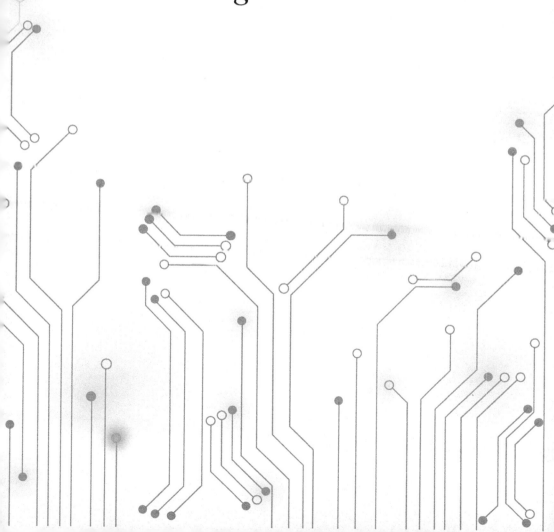

MIND:
"Angel lta. . . ."

Why should we read?

△ CHILD

Reading is an important part of learning. It helps you understand the world around you and helps you remember things. When you read, you can explore different places and learn about different people and cultures. Reading can also help you express your thoughts and feelings and give you new ideas. It can also help you become a better writer and speaker. Finally, reading can be a fun and relaxing way to pass the time.

△DULT VERSION

Reading is an important part of learning and personal growth. It helps to improve language skills, increase knowledge, and even reduce stress. Reading can also be a great way to relax and escape from the stresses of daily life. Reading can help to broaden our perspective, give us new ideas, and help us to think critically. Reading can also help to develop empathy as we get to know characters and explore their situations. Lastly, reading is a great way to increase vocabulary and improve writing skills.

HUMAN

Reading exercises the mind and can take you on an adventure at the same time. Something to read can lead you on a journey away from your consciousness as does sleep, only you are in an awakened state. Reading can bring the world's historical past and present triumphs and failures into your perception and memory. Learning to process ideas creates an opportunity to think outside of yourself.

The huamn mnid deos not raed ervey lteter by istlef. It raesd the wrod as a wlohe.

Why should we write?

△ CHILD

Writing is a great way to express yourself and your ideas. When you write, you can use words to tell stories, explain things, and share your thoughts. Writing can help you remember things better, organize your thoughts, and even come up with new ideas. Writing can also help you practice communicating with others, which is important in life. Writing can be a lot of fun too!

△DULT VERSION

Writing is an essential tool for communication and self-expression. It allows us to create and share ideas, express our emotions, tell stories, and even record our history. Writing can also help us process and make sense of our thoughts and experiences, and it can be a great form of self-care and personal growth. Writing can also help us connect with others and build relationships, as it can serve as a powerful medium for exchanging and understanding different perspectives.

HUMAN

If something is going to write for us, aren't we giving it the power to think for us? All technology can be used as a helpful tool, but it's going to be integrated into our word processing programs. Even if humans have the choice (in settings) to turn it on/off, children learning to write won't have the foresight to learn to write on their own first:

Pre-internet, scribes, books, schools,
Internet, bribes, CPUs, fools,
AI, tribes, slaves, ghouls:
Hand and eye
Must script the mind.
Restore the pen
To avoid a fen.

*The FWORD is mightier than the SWORD, but is it mightier than
Reactive Machine, Limited Memory, Theory of Mind, and Self-aware AI?*

Why should we calculate?

△ CHILD

Math is an important skill that helps us understand the world around us. Math helps us to understand how things work and how to solve problems. We use math to figure out how much things cost, how to measure things, and how to make things work. Math also helps us understand how things like computers and phones work. Math is an important skill that helps us understand a lot of different things, so it's important to learn it.

△DULT VERSION

Math is an essential life skill that can help people understand the world around them. It enables people to make sense of patterns, relationships, and how things work, which can help them gain a better understanding of the world. Math also teaches problem-solving skills, which can be very useful in real-life situations. Doing math can also help people become better at logical thinking and creative problem-solving, which can be beneficial in many aspects of life, such as work and school.

HUMAN

Math doesn't seem human at all, but logical thought is important for all aspects of life. Again, math doesn't seem human, yet many of us assign meaning to numbers. What if this book came into existence because its human author kept seeing certain groups of numbers? Which led to angel numbers, which led to a drawing of a little angel, which led to Angelita? And then there's the infinite monkey theorem. Calculations have been taken over by calculators, computers, and phones. As humans, we need to exercise and strengthen our logical minds with such things as math and games like chess. We are not mere algorithms.

2+2=5 is a warning, and pie tastes like the universe.

Why should we think?

△ CHILD

A person should think because it helps them make good decisions. Thinking helps us ask questions, consider different options, and come up with the best solution. It's important to think before you make any decision, big or small. Thinking helps us understand the world around us and the people in it. It also helps us develop our skills and knowledge. Thinking is an important part of life, and it's something that everyone should do.

△DULT VERSION

A person should think because it is the key to developing sound judgement, formulating thoughtful opinions, and making sound decisions. Thinking helps us to analyze and interpret the world around us, paving the way for us to make informed decisions. Thinking also helps us to develop problem-solving skills, which can he applied to various aspects of life. In addition, thinking helps us to gain insight into ourselves and our environment, enabling us to better understand and appreciate our place in the world. Finally, thinking can help us to develop creative solutions to problems and to become more productive in our lives.

HUMAN

Cogito, ergo sum, "I think, therefore I am" is from the philosopher, scientist, and mathematician René Descartes. Well, maybe he did and maybe he didn't. The point is this: do the math. You're going to need lots of practice thinking, and the best way to think is by reading, calculating, and just plain old daydreaming and imagining.

"*AI thinks, therefore it is, but it ain't!*" *Think for yourself and your self.*

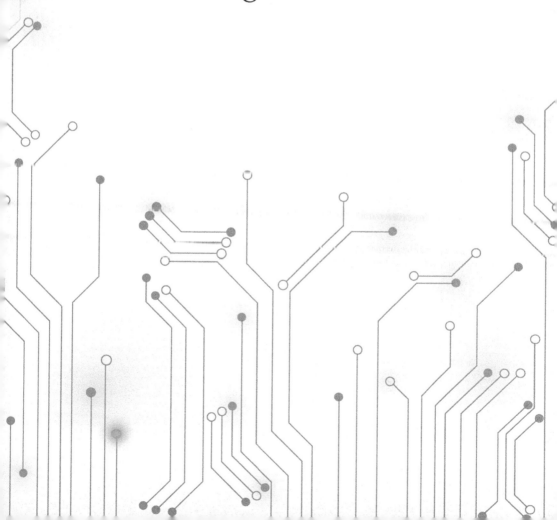

SOUL:
"Angel1ta..."

What is life?

△ CHILD

Life is a journey of experiences and growth. It is how we learn and grow, make mistakes and learn from them, and how we appreciate the good times and use the bad times to make ourselves stronger. Life is about creating relationships, exploring the world, discovering our passions and interests, and finding our place in the world.

△DULT VERSION

Life is an experience that is unique to every individual. It is the process of living, growing, and learning through interactions with the world. It is a journey that includes joy, happiness, sorrow, and pain. Life is a precious gift that should be cherished and enjoyed.

HUMAN

> "Hey, Brian. Guess where I am?"
> "Where?"
> "I'm at the cemetery at my future gravesite."
> "My God, this guy's at his grave!"
> (*laughter and amazement*)

This actual and real conversation was a long, long time ago when I was barely out of my teenage years. Since then, my father has been buried there. If it wasn't a reminder back in my early 20s . . . my father's life certainly drove the point home: it is never too early to contemplate your own life; it can lead to strength, understanding, fearlessness, and endless epiphanic revelations.

Before life is death, and death leads to life, and life leads to after life.

What is death?

A CHILD

Death is when someone's body stops working. It happens to everyone eventually and it is part of life. When someone dies, they cannot come back, and we feel sad because we miss them.

ADULT VERSION

Death is the permanent cessation of all biological functions that sustain a living organism. It is the end of an organism's life, a final event from which no organism can recover. Death is often viewed as a sad or unpleasant occurrence, though, depending on the circumstances, it may also be welcomed as a relief from suffering.

HUMAN

"Hey, Brian. Guess where he's at?"
"Where?"
"He's at the cemetery at his gravesite."
"My God, this guy's in his grave."
(*sadness and amazement*)

I will never have this conversation. This fictional conversation was altered for this book in 2023. Before then, my father was buried there. If it isn't a reminder now . . . my father's death certainly drives the point home: it is never too early to contemplate your own death; it can lead to strength, understanding, fearlessness, and endless epiphanic revelations.

Before death leads to life, and life leads to death, and death leads to after death.

What is the Universe?

A CHILD

The universe is everything that exists. It includes stars, planets, galaxies, and all the empty space between them. The universe is so big that we may never be able to explore it all. It is constantly expanding, so it is always getting bigger!

ADULT VERSION

The universe is the totality of all space, time, matter, energy, and the physical laws and constants that govern them. It is the sum of all that exists, including stars, galaxies, planets, moons, black holes, quasars, and all other forms of matter and energy. It is an incredibly vast and complex system, and its size and composition are constantly changing.

HUMAN

The Universe is all and nothing and everything in between; it's safe to say no one knows for sure until they're dead . . . maybe.

Some say the universe and perhaps the soul of a person can be seen in the eyes.

There is also something to be said about the idea that going along and redirecting yourself as things in life challenge what *you* see as *your* path, might be the best way to "go with the flow," so to speak. Many humans seem to find peace in allowing events to play out as "the universe" dictates. There's also the idea that the past and future don't exist, perhaps, and everything has already happened. The present is always now, so why waste your time worrying?

Read all the books, see all the shows. Truth be told, nobody knows. Beware of those somebodies who say they do, traverse the verse for me and you.

Who is God?

⟁ CHILD

God is like a loving parent who is always there for you and loves you very much. He watches over you and cares for you no matter what, and He is always with you. He is a powerful and wise being that created the whole universe and all of the amazing things in it. He is always looking out for you and wants the best for you.

⟁DULT VERSION

God is the creator and sustainer of the universe, a being of infinite power, knowledge, and love. He is the ultimate source of truth, justice, and morality and is the ultimate judge of all mankind. He is often described as having a personality, with the capacity to interact with humans, to hear and answer prayers, and to forgive sin.

HUMAN

He, She, the Entity: God is all and nothing and everything in between; it's safe to say no one knows for sure until they're dead . . . maybe.

God help us!
AI who?
Artificial Intelligence.
Who's there?
Click. Click.
Knock. Knock.

Who's there?
God.
God who?
God we wish we knew.
God you have no clue.
God I hope it's you.

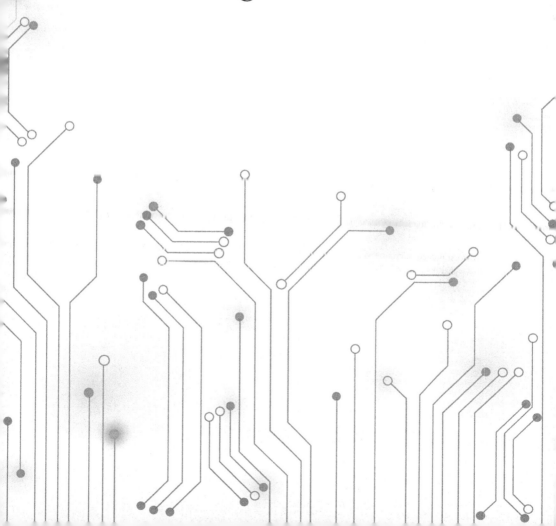

DEED:
"Angellta..."

Why is it important to go outside?

△ CH▯LD

Going outside is important because it gives you the chance to explore the world around you. When you go outside, you get to see different plants and animals, feel the wind on your skin, and breathe in the fresh air. Going outside also helps you get exercise, which is important for your health. Being outside can also help you relax and clear your mind, so it's a great way to relieve stress.

△DULT VERS▯ON

Going outside is important for a variety of reasons. Physically, it can help us to maintain a healthy lifestyle by providing opportunities to get exercise and fresh air. Mentally, being outside can reduce stress levels and boost mood, while providing a sense of connection to nature. Going outside can also provide social benefits, as being around other people can help to increase self-esteem and promote positive relationships. On a larger scale, going outside can help us to appreciate our environment and the importance of protecting it.

HUMAN

No mention of the sun. The sun! A sin not to mention the sun! Go outside because the sun is out there. The light is out there. We need the light on our human faces. We are solar powered.

Go outside your comfort zone, and never return.

How do I make my mind quiet?

A CHILD

It can be hard to quiet your mind, especially when you are feeling overwhelmed. Here are some things that can help: 1. Take some deep breaths. Close your eyes and take slow, deep breaths in and out. This can help you to relax and focus. 2. Picture a peaceful place. Imagine a place that you feel safe and relaxed in. It could be a beach, a garden, or even a room in your house. 3. Listen to calming music. Put on some soothing music, close your eyes, and focus on the sounds. 4. Write down your thoughts. Writing down your thoughts can help to clear your mind and make it easier to focus. 5. Take a break. Spend some time away from screens, phones, and other distractions. Go for a walk, do some yoga, or do a craft. These are some of the ways to help calm your mind and make it quiet. It takes practice, but with time you will get better at it.

ADULT VERSION

1. Take a few deep breaths. Close your eyes and focus on your breathing, simply noticing the sensation of the air entering and exiting your lungs. 2. Release any thoughts that enter your mind. Accept that they are there, but do not engage with them. 3. If you find yourself getting distracted, refocus your attention on your breath. 4. Engage in meditation or mindfulness exercises. 5. Focus on peaceful thoughts or images. Visualize a calming scene or phrase. 6. Practice progressive muscle relaxation. Starting from your toes, tense and then relax each muscle group in your body. 7. Take time for yourself. Spend a few minutes each day in

quiet, alone time. 8. Practice yoga or tai chi to relax your body and mind. 9. Listen to calming music. 10. Engage in other activities to help you relax and quiet your mind, such as listening to a guided meditation, reading a book, or going for a walk.

HUMAN

Open your eyes but close them. Close your eyes but keep them open. Don't think of anything or think of something so intensely that eventually you grow bored of it. The mind will then simply drift away for a moment, or maybe longer, into a quiet place. Don't try to quiet your mind. It will quiet itself. If none of that works, tire yourself out mentally and physically then rest and think of the entire universe. Delete stars, planets, solar systems, one by one, then delete the blackness that remains. What's left? What do you see? Delete that . . .

Shhhhhhh . . .

What should I do if I am sad and lonely?

△ CHILD

If you're feeling lonely or sad, it's important to talk to someone you trust about how you're feeling. It could be a parent, teacher, or another adult you know. Talking to someone can help you feel better and figure out how to make things better. You can also try to do something that makes you feel better, such as playing with a pet, reading a book, or coloring.

△DULT VERSION

If you are feeling lonely or sad, it is important to reach out to your friends and family. Spend time with people who make you feel loved and supported. You can also find support groups online or in person where you can talk to people who may be going through similar experiences. Additionally, it may be helpful to engage in activities that make you feel good, such as exercise, journaling, or taking a walk. Finally, if you feel like you need more help, make sure to reach out to a mental health professional.

HUMAN

Experience those feelings as if water were running on your hands and between your fingers. Then clean them and dry them off. Someone or something is always with you. Every human feels sad or lonely at some point, which declares sadness and loneliness are nothing to fear.

Feel your feelings and you will get used to each other.

How do I find my purpose?

A CHILD

Purpose in life is like a compass—it can help guide you in the right direction. When you find your purpose, it means you've discovered what's important to you, and it gives you direction and focus in your life. To find your purpose, think about what's important to you and what makes you happy. Ask yourself questions like: What activities make me feel energized and excited? What would I do if I had unlimited time and money? What skills do I have that I can use to help others? Then, look for ways to turn those passions into something meaningful. You could volunteer your time, pursue a career that fits your interests, or start a project that makes a difference in your community. When you discover your purpose, you'll have something to focus on and strive towards.

Adult version

A person can find purpose in their life by exploring their interests and passions, setting personal goals, and taking action towards achieving them. It can also be helpful to reflect on the values that are important to them, and consider how their choices can align with those values. Additionally, connecting with other people and engaging in meaningful relationships can bring purpose and fulfillment to life. Other strategies for finding purpose include volunteering, pursuing creative activities, and engaging in spiritual or religious practices.

HUMAN

You've heard this before: your purpose in life is to live. Live life to its fullest in everything single moment and every single breath be it deep or shallow.

Carpe diem. Everyone serves a purpose; therefore, your purpose will be found when it serves you, perhaps even by serving others.

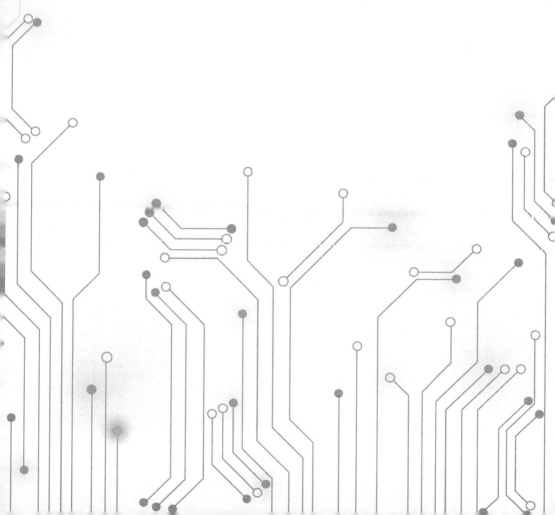

LOVE:
"Angel Ita . . ."

What is love?

△ CHILD

Love is a feeling of strong affection and care for someone. It's like a warm hug that makes you feel safe and happy. When you love someone, you want what's best for them and you want to be with them and make them happy.

△DULT VERSION

Love is an intense feeling of affection and care for another person. It is a deep emotional bond that is both powerful and positive. Love can be felt for family, friends, partners, pets, and even inanimate objects. It is a complex emotion that is both universal and personal, and it can be expressed through many different acts of kindness, from compliments to physical touch.

HUMAN

Thousands of stories, poems, letters, and lyrics have been written about it, and still, no one has the faintest idea of the nature of love; I got nothing.

Maybe love's perfection presents itself in moments and memories, not necessarily long lengths and lifetimes, yet it surely stands the test of time. Arguably, the culture who best defined love were (and are) the Greeks:

Agape: unconditional love
Eros: sexual desire

Ludus:	playful love
Mania:	obsessive love
Meraki:	creative endeavors
Philautia:	self-love
Philia:	soul connection
Pragma:	mature love
Storge:	devoted love

If you experience any of these in your lifetime, it's a gift. Here's a prose and mildly poetic example of how someone might experience all-of-the-above in a rant to love itself:

"O hear me beautiful One!
Forgive me my rants.
I know not what I say or chant.
I'm passion, wild,
A tantrum child!"

She finally shows herself to him.
He feels her blushing on his skin
As her shy beauty peeked around
Like the sun past a summer cloud.

I jibber-jabber when I'm out amongst people when you're not there to pass the time . . .
Because otherwise, I'd be quiet.

You grow each day in your life until its end, while I rave-rattle to anyone who will listen . . .
Otherwise, I'd be quiet.

I scream how I would lightly and firmly and every-type-of-touch-you public and private, the bronzed, pale, and pink parts of you. If I didn't know otherwise . . .
I'd be quiet.

I yell to the universe, "Who has this much passion and yearning to experience you?" as the ebb and flow of time washes away opportunity. If only I'd . . .
Be quiet.

Be "Yours!" and . . .
Quiet.
Love verses poetry and poetry verses love.

What is the best way to choose a partner?

A CHILD

The best way to choose a partner is to find someone who you respect, trust, and enjoy spending time with. It should be someone who shares your values and beliefs, and someone who you can talk to easily and openly. It's also important to make sure that you feel comfortable and safe when you're around them.

ADULT VERSION

The best way to choose a partner is to take your time and be mindful of the qualities you are looking for. Consider the type of relationship you are looking for and the qualities in a partner you believe will make a successful and healthy relationship. Evaluate potential partners through meaningful conversations and activities to get to know them and their values, goals, and beliefs. Spend time with them to figure out if they are compatible with you, and be honest and open with them about your expectations. Make sure to take a step back and reflect on your feelings and the experiences you have together. Ultimately, choose someone who makes you feel safe, supported, and happy.

HUMAN

Somewhere deep inside us, we all just want to be loved. Many of us fail at seeing all the people and things in nature that do love us already. A partner can be a person, a pet, or nature. As you read this, you know, you just know, you have love for all things wonderful, and you can be sure there are enough wonderful things in the world to love you back. Live in the moments.

A partner can last for a long time, for a short time, for a moment, but every choice you make is a choice you loved.

What is the most important thing about being human?

A CHILD

The most important thing about being human is that we have the ability to think and make choices. We can use our minds to create, solve problems, and help others. We can use our hearts to care for each other and show love and kindness. Being human also means that we have the ability to learn and grow, so that we can become the best version of ourselves.

ADULT VERSION

The most important thing about being human is having the capacity to think, reason, and make conscious choices. Having the ability to reason and make decisions allows us to make plans, create solutions to problems, and develop relationships with others. It also allows us to empathize with others and understand our own emotions, which can lead to better communication and understanding. Ultimately, being human means having the ability to make deliberate choices and take responsibility for the consequences that come with them.

HUMAN

Interesting that the AI adult version overlooks the words "love and kindness." Do we lose the ability as adults to have or show empathy toward others simply because the world's work-program, the world's software is designed or accidentally designed to delete such things? In computer jargon, humans are the hardware.

Hardware is a rock without software. Humanity without software is extinct. Program yourself with BASIC:

```
10 PRINT "Love and Kindness"
20 GOTO 10
] RUN
```
Love and Kindness
Love and Kindness
Love and Kindness
Love and Kindness . . .

What does it mean to be nice?

A CHILD

Being nice means being kind, friendly, and respectful to other people. It means treating others the way you want to be treated. It means being generous and helpful. It means being understanding and patient. It means being polite and showing appreciation for the things other people do for us.

ADULT VERSION

Being nice is about treating others with kindness and respect. It means being friendly and considerate, and thinking of how your actions might affect other people. It also means showing empathy and understanding and taking the time to listen to others. Being nice is about creating an atmosphere of positivity and helping to make the world a better place.

HUMAN

Remember things: big, little, lasting, fleeting. People that pass through your life and how you treat them are all that's important. No one's perfect and everyone makes mistakes: most of us know this. Even when we're driving, most of us know this!

Then there's that moment when you get angry about some issue or problem. When you're young, you act and talk like a raging runt, go in mouth-hazing and perhaps fist-pounding, recklessly playing the odds.

46

Later in life, you might just become frustrated to the point of submission. Sometimes apathy will be the response to an on-going issue, and many times, the more patient ones, wait it out until they can flee the problem, or the problem itself dissolves or dies, or maybe you die.

Though, every now and then, a whisper grows wings, and its ascensive scaling becomes a vine and voice, and then no longer a trembling, troubled, and treble note, but soon a booming, bass, and euphonic letter, word, and message that reaches out to the world: "Be nice. Be nice for cryin' out loud. For the love of God and the Universe, be nice."

A sad . . . scared . . . starving child . . . be nice.

. . . 16th century—present
The Tragedy of HamNet
Act I, Scene iii
I,III

I,3

I3

"This above all:

mind thine
As and Is."

Made in the USA
Columbia, SC
29 April 2023

15932467R00037